Anne of Green Gables

Study Guide

by Alisa Thomas

Limited permission to reproduce this study guide

Anne of Green Gables Study Guide
A Progeny Press Study Guide
by Alisa Thomas
edited by Rebecca Gilleland and Michael S. Gilleland
cover design by Michael S. Gilleland

Printed in the United States of America.

ISBN:978-1-58609-331-0 Book
        978-1-58609-582-6 CD
        978-1-58609-423-2 Set

Study Guide Author

Alisa Thomas currently serves as Instructor of English at Toccoa Falls College in Georgia, and has ministered through teaching at the University of Louisville and the Christian Academy of Louisville in Kentucky. Ms. Thomas graduated from Georgetown College, Georgetown, Kentucky, with a double major in American Studies and English. She completed her Master of Arts in English at the University of Louisville. Her thesis, "Ephemeral Quests for Autonomy," examined the spiritual implications of Nathaniel Hawthorne's depictions of childhood experience from an interdisciplinary perspective.

Peer Review Panel

The Rev. Michael S. Poteet is an ordained minister in the Presbyterian Church (USA), currently pastoring a congregation in Clifton Heights, Pennsylvania. A native Texan, Mr. Poteet earned an undergraduate degree in English and Religion at the College of William and Mary in Virginia and earned his Masters of Divinity degree at Princeton Theological Seminary. In addition to writing for Progeny Press, Mr. Poteet also is an aspiring science fiction writer; his first professionally published short story appeared in *Star Trek: Strange New Worlds II* (Pocket Books, May 1999). He is married and has one child.

Calvin Roso is a full-time instructor at Oral Roberts University and consults Christian schools in the area of curriculum design and evaluation. He has taught high school English for nine years and teaches workshops in the United States and Latin America on the topics of literature and curriculum. In addition to writing several study guides, Mr. Roso has published a number of articles on curriculum for Christian schools. He earned his Bachelor's Degree in English Education from the University of Wisconsin—Madison and a Master's Degree in Education from Oral Roberts University, where he is currently pursuing a Doctorate in Education.

Peer Review Panel membership as of August 2001.

Table of Contents

Note to Instructor

How to Use Progeny Press Study Guides.   Progeny Press study guides are designed to help students better understand and enjoy literature by getting them to notice and understand how authors craft their stories and to show them how to think through the themes and ideas introduced in the stories. To properly work through a Progeny Press study guide, students should have easy access to a good dictionary, a thesaurus, a Bible (we use NIV translation, but that is up to your preference; just be aware of some differences in language), and sometimes a topical Bible or concordance. Supervised access to the Internet also can be helpful at times, as can a good set of encyclopedias.

Most middle grades and high school study guides take from eight to ten weeks to complete, generally working on one section per week. Over the years, we have found that it works best if the students completely read the novel the first week, while also working on a prereading activity chosen by the parent or teacher. Starting the second week, most parents and teachers have found it works best to work on one study guide page per day until the chapter sections are completed. Students should be allowed to complete questions by referring to the book; many questions require some cross-reference between elements of the stories.

Most study guides contain an Overview section that can be used as a final test, or it can be completed in the same way the chapter sections were completed. If you wish to perform a final test but your particular study guide does not have an Overview section, we suggest picking a couple of questions from each section of the study guide and using them as your final test.

Most study guides also have a final section of essays and postreading activities. These may be assigned at the parents' or teachers' discretion, but we suggest that students engage in several writing or other extra activities during the study of the novel to complement their reading and strengthen their writing skills.

As for high school credits, most Christian high schools with whom we have spoken have assigned a value of one-fourth credit to each study guide, and this also seems to be acceptable to colleges assessing homeschool transcripts.

Internet References

All websites listed in this study guide were checked for appropriateness at the time of publication. However, due to the changing nature of the Internet, we cannot guarantee that the URLs listed will remain appropriate or viable. Therefore, we urge parents and teachers to take care in and exercise careful oversight of their children's use of the Internet.

Synopsis

When Marilla Cuthbert and her brother Matthew send for an orphan boy to help Matthew on the farm, Anne Shirley, a skinny, red-headed girl who never stops talking, arrives instead.

From the beginning, Matthew's heart is captured by this "kindred spirit" and he decides he wants to keep her. Marilla reluctantly agrees to this, but eventually finds herself absorbed by Anne's chatter, amused by the scrapes Anne gets herself into, and frustrated with Anne always having her head in the clouds.

As Anne grows, Marilla finds her a "genius for getting into trouble"; yet, as Anne says, "have you ever noticed one encouraging thing about me, Marilla? I never make the same mistake twice." Despite her many predicaments, life at Green Gables is happy.

Anne becomes wiser and steadier with age, making Marilla and Matthew proud of her many accomplishments. Only when tragedy strikes Green Gables does Marilla finally admit how much Anne is part of her life, and how very much she loves her.

About the Novel's Author

Well, I've written my book [Anne of Green Gables]. The dream dreamed years ago in that old brown desk in school has come true at last after years of toil and struggle. And the realization is sweet—almost as sweet as the dream!

Lucy Maud Montgomery was born November 30, 1874. Almost like Anne, Montgomery lost her mother when she was barely out of infancy and was raised by her grandparents on Prince Edward Island. While briefly residing with her father and her stepmother, she had to leave school for periods to help with household tasks. After deciding to return to Prince Edward Island, she had to readjust herself to live within the rigid boundaries of her grandparents.

Montgomery discovered a creative outlet through writing. Her first published work was a poem ("On Cape Le Force") for the Charlottetown *Daily Patriot* in 1890. She continued to write articles and poems while completing her studies. Montgomery was awarded distinctions for work in English, agriculture, and "school management." She also attended Dalhousie College for one year.

In 1905, Montgomery began writing her most famous book, *Anne of Green Gables*. The novel was published in 1908. *Anne of Green Gables* met with enthusiastic response, and 19,000 copies were sold during a six-month span. The novel's sequel, *Anne of Avonlea,* was published in 1909. Montgomery continued the series with *Anne of the Island* (1913) and *Anne's House of Dreams* (1917). In 1911, she married Ewan Macdonald, a Presbyterian minister. They had two children, Chester (1912) and Ewan (1915).

Montgomery's love for Prince Edward Island is reflected in her fiction. The author's family had lived on Prince Edward Island since the 1700s, and as an adult, Montgomery sketched the inhabitants of her childhood community as "loyal, clannish, upright, God-fearing, inheriting traditions of faith and simplicity and aspiration."

Montgomery died in 1942.

Optional Pre-reading Activities

1. Draw a map of Prince Edward Island, the setting of *Anne of Green Gables*. Indicate key geographical features of the region, including the following locations, on your map.
   —Gulf of St. Lawrence
   —Northumberland Strait
   —North Cape
   —East Point
   —Cardigan Bay
   —Rocky Point

2. "I've been reading *Waverley* this evening. Splendid old Scott! His magic never fails. After a surfeit of glittering, empty modern fiction I always come back to him as to some tired old friend who never fails to charm. What a delight the few novels of Scott which I could get to read in early life were to me!"

    L.M. Montgomery's favorite author was Sir Walter Scott. Name your favorite author and titles that "delight" you.

3. Write a one-page report about Prince Edward Island.

4. Do some research into orphanages of the late 1800s and early 1900s. Why were they created? Who ran them? What were living conditions like? Write a one- or two-page report about your findings.

Chapters 1–4

Vocabulary:

A word is *in context* if we see it in the sentence in which it was written. It is *out of context* when the word is by itself. Consider how each underlined vocabulary word is used in context. Write a brief definition of each term in your own words. Compare your definition to the dictionary definition.

1. "But by the time it reached Lynde's Hollow it was a quiet well-conducted little stream, for not even a brook could run past Mrs. Rachel Lynde's door without due regard for decency and <u>decorum</u>. . . ."
   Your definition:

   Dictionary definition:

2. "The sun was coming in at the window warm and bright; the orchard on the slope below the house was in a bridal flush of pinky-white bloom, hummed over by a <u>myriad</u> of bees."
   Your definition:

   Dictionary definition:

3. "Very green and neat and precise was that yard, set about on one side with great <u>patriarchal</u> willows and on the other with prim Lombardies."
   Your definition:

   Dictionary definition:

4. "Matthew is getting up in years, you know—he's sixty—and he isn't so <u>spry</u> as he once was."
    Your definition:

    Dictionary definition:

5. "[A]n extraordinary observer might have seen that the chin was pointed and pronounced; that the big eyes were full of spirit and vivacity; that the mouth was sweet-lipped and expressive; that the forehead was broad and full; in short, our <u>discerning</u> extraordinary observer might have concluded that no common-place soul inhabited the body of this stray woman-child of whom shy Matthew Cuthbert was so <u>ludicrously</u> afraid."

    discerning:
    Your definition:

    Dictionary definition:

    ludicrously:
    Your definition:

    Dictionary definition:

6. "I read of a girl once in a novel who had a lifelong sorrow but it wasn't red hair. Her hair was pure gold, rippling back from her <u>alabaster</u> brow."
    Your definition:

    Dictionary definition:

7. "The 'Avenue,' so called by the Newbridge people, was a stretch of road four or five hundred yards long, completely arched over by huge wide-spreading apple-trees, planted years ago by an <u>eccentric</u> old farmer.
    Your definition:

    Dictionary definition:

8. "She came out of her <u>reverie</u> with a deep sigh and looked at him with the dreamy gaze of a soul that had been wondering afar, star-led."
    Your definition:

    Dictionary definition:

9. "Marilla came briskly forward as Matthew opened the door. But when her eyes fell on the odd little figure in the stiff ugly dress, with the long braids of red hair and the eager, <u>luminous</u> eyes, she stopped short in amazement."
    Your definition:

    Dictionary definition:

Questions:

1. Briefly describe each of the four main characters we have met so far: Anne, Marilla, Matthew, and Rachel.

2. Why do Marilla and Matthew decide to bring an orphan boy to Green Gables?

3. Why does Rachel disapprove of this plan?

4. Anne is a very optimistic person. Define *optimism*. Give one example from the book showing Anne's optimism.

5. How does Marilla react when Anne arrives instead of the expected boy? Why?

6. Why does Matthew feel that Anne should remain at Green Gables?

7. Beyond telling Marilla that they should keep Anne, what does Matthew *do* to keep Anne?

Thinking About the Story:

8. Authors use colorful and descriptive language to give the reader a "picture in words." Choose two descriptive words from the quote and use them in your own sentence.

    > "Above the bridge the pond ran up into fringing groves of fir and maple and lay all darkly translucent in their wavering shadows. Here and there a wild plum leaned out from the bank like a white-clad girl tiptoeing to her own reflection. From the marsh at the head of the pond came the clear, mournfully sweet chorus of the frogs."

    Optional: Adjectives are words that describe a noun. Therefore, any word describing a person, place, or thing is usually an adjective. Underline adjectives in the quote above.

9. A *simile* is a figure of speech used to describe something through comparison. A simile uses words such as *like* or *as* to indicate that a comparison is taking place. For example: "The moss-covered rocks looked *like* green velvet pillows scattered around the glen." Identify the simile used in the following sentence. Rewrite this sentence with a simile of your own, comparing the wild plum to something else.

    > "Here and there a wild plum leaned out from the bank like a white-clad girl tiptoeing to her own reflection."

10. Look up Exodus 22:22–24; Psalm 146:9; and James 1:27. Summarize how God deals with orphans.

Dig Deeper:

11. Read Genesis 2:8–9; Psalm 19:1–4; Psalm 33:6–7; Psalm 148. What do these Bible verses teach us about God's creation?

12. When Matthew and Marilla first meet Anne, they have very different experiences. Briefly describe how Matthew gets to know Anne, then briefly describe Marilla's first experiences with Anne. Do you think Matthew and Marilla had the same or different attitudes toward Anne at the end of their first night together? How do you think these first experiences shaped their impressions of Anne? Do you think their reactions are justified considering their first impressions?

13. Matthew feels that they should keep Anne, not because of what she could do for them, but because they might do some good for her. Read Luke 10:30–37. Compare this parable with Matthew's experiences with Anne. How are Anne and Matthew like the people in the parable, and how does Matthew embody Jesus' last instruction?

Optional Activities:

1. One of L.M. Montgomery's most important sources for *Anne of Green Gables* was a feature story about an orphan. Find a story in a newspaper or magazine that could serve as the basis for a story. Write an imaginative one-to-three page short story based on it.

2. If the time of year is right, gather some apple or plum blossoms and put them in a large vase to admire as you read *Anne of Green Gables*. If apple and plum trees are not in bloom, pick other flowers, or gather pictures of flowers from catalogs or magazines and create an attractive display. You may wish to add an apple-scented candle or potpourri to your display.

3. Bring in a potted geranium or other flowering plant and pick a name for it.

4. Using paints or colored pencils, create a picture of the "White Way of Delight," or create a pencil drawing of the east gable room.

Chapters 5–10

Vocabulary:

Define each word, then use it in a sentence.

1. **benevolent**
    Definition:

    Sentence:

2. **blight**
    Definition:

    Sentence:

3. **harrowed**
    Definition:

    Sentence:

4. **tremulous**
    Definition:

    Sentence:

5. **penitent**
Definition:

Sentence:

6. **deprecation**
Definition:

Sentence:

7. **indignation**
Definition:

Sentence:

8. **amiable**
Definition:

Sentence:

9. **abasement**
Definition:

Sentence:

10. **plaintive**
Definition:

Sentence:

Questions:

1. Anne tells Marilla, "It's been my experience that you can nearly always enjoy things if you make up your mind firmly that you will." Do you agree? Why or why not?

2. When Marilla asks Anne if Mrs. Thomas and Mrs. Hammond were good to her, how does Anne respond?

3. Why doesn't Anne speak ill of Mrs. Thomas and Mrs. Hammond when she would be justified in saying they were not good to her?

4. Anne states that she desires to pray in "a great big field all alone or into the deep, deep woods. . . ." Why do you think Anne favors this location? Where is your favorite place to pray?

5. Who were the two friends from Anne's past that she tells Marilla about? Where did she "see" them?

6. Why does Anne finally agree to apologize to Rachel?

7. Is Anne genuinely sorry for her behavior? Explain why you think she was or was not.

Think About the Story:

8. When Anne asks Marilla whether she ever imagines things "'different from what they really are,'" Marilla responds, "'I don't believe in imagining things different from what they really are. . . . When the Lord puts us in certain circumstances He doesn't mean for us to imagine them away.'" Do you agree with Marilla that God does not want us to ever imagine things different from the way they are? Why or why not? Are there appropriate and inappropriate times for imagining things different?

9. Marilla tells Anne that they will keep her "provided she tries to be good and grateful." Do you think this leaves Anne feeling very secure? Why or why not? How good or grateful does she have to be for them to keep her?

10. Marilla realizes that Anne "cares nothing about God's love since she has never had it translated to her through the medium of human love." Read Matthew 25:34–40; Colossians 3:12–17; 1 John 3:16–18; 4:10, 11. How are we to demonstrate God's love to others? How?

11. Compare and contrast the wagon ride Matthew takes with Anne in Chapter 2 with the wagon ride Anne takes with Marilla in Chapters 5 and 6. What happens on the rides and what is the result of the rides?

12. An *allusion* is a reference to historical or fictional people, places, events, or statements that the author assumes will be recognized by the reader. In the middle of Chapter 8, Montgomery alludes to a duchess:

> Marilla was as fond of morals as the Duchess in Wonderland, and was firmly convinced that one should be tacked on to every remark made to a child who was being brought up.

Who is the "Duchess in Wonderland"? What was she like, and what might Montgomery be saying about Marilla by alluding to the Duchess?

Dig Deeper:

13. Anne has not had a very stable or secure life so far; sometimes life can be very insecure. Read Psalm 18:1–2; Romans 8:31, 35, 37–39. In what can we always feel secure?

14. When Rachel first meets Anne, she says, "'She's terrible skinny and homely, Marilla. Come here, child, and let me have a look at you. Lawful heart, did any one ever see such freckles? And hair as red as carrots!'" Why does Rachel feel free to "speak her mind" in Anne's presence?

15. Read Ephesians 4:15, 29, and 32. According to these verses, how should we speak truth to others? Does what Rachel says to Anne fit these verse? Why or why not?

16. Marilla tells Anne that although Rachel was too outspoken, it did *not* excuse Anne's behavior. What reasons did she give for demanding that Anne respect Rachel? Read Luke 6:27–36. Paraphrase these verses. How do these verses compare with Marilla's requirements?

17. Think of a time when someone hurt your feelings. How did you respond to the situation? How should you have responded?

18. At the end of Chapter 10 Anne says, "Saying one's prayers isn't exactly the same thing as praying." What do you think she means by this? Do you agree with her?

Optional Activities:

1. L.M. Montgomery wrote of her deep affection for Prince Edward Island. The following passage comes from a journal entry dated June 1, 1909.

   The tall slender firs along the moist red road came out against it in a grace and beauty that made me ache for joy; and behind me a full moon deepened until the white radiance mingled with the gold and flame of the west.

   Anne also finds delight and inspiration in the natural wonders of Prince Edward Island.

   Anne had made good use of every waking moment of that fortnight. Already she was acquainted with every tree and shrub about the place. She had discovered that a lane opened out below the apple orchard and ran up through a belt of woodland; and she had explored it to its farthest end in all its delicious vagaries of brook and bridge, fir coppice and wild cherry arch, corners thick with fern, and branching byways of maple and mountain ash.

Write a paragraph describing your favorite place. Use vivid descriptive language to bring this scene to life. Why is this location meaningful to you?

2. Imagine you are Anne at the end of Chapter 10 and you are praying at the gable window. What would you pray? Write down your prayer. You may wish to decorate the margins of your page in an appropriate manner to match the prayer.

3. There are a number of scenes in these chapters that could be very funny (for instance, when Anne prays for the first time, "Poor Marilla was only preserved from complete collapse by remembering that it was not irreverence, but simply spiritual ignorance . . . that was responsible for this extraordinary petition."). Look through Chapters 5–10 and find such a scene to act out. Make the most of the humor.

Chapters 11–15

Vocabulary:

A *synonym* is a word that has the same or almost same meaning as another word. The words in each clue list below are synonyms for the missing word. Fill in the blank with the word from the Word Box that most closely matches the meaning of the words in the clue list.

Word Box

resolute	disdainfully	brusquely	mortified
sublime	bequeathed	candidly	sallow
beguiled	tantalize	contritely	vindictive

humiliated
vexed
embarrassed

1. _____

yellow
wan
unhealthy

2. _____

noble
lofty
magnificent

3. _____

interest
excite
captivate

4. _____

deceive
cheat
charm

5. _____

contemptuously
scornfully
condescendingly

6. _____

stubborn
determined
fixed

7. _____

gave
bestowed
handed down

8. _____

shortly
abruptly
bluntly

9. _____

fairly	vengeful	grieving
frankly	spiteful	sorry
honestly	unforgiving	penitently

10. _____   11. _____   12. _____

Questions:

1. Why is Anne disappointed with the dresses that Marilla provides? How does she resolve this dilemma?

2. Although Anne says some things about church and Sunday School that Marilla disapproves of, Marilla does not reprove Anne. Why not?

3. When Matthew gives Anne some chocolates, what does she do with them?

4. Why is Anne grounded from attending the church picnic?

5. Who calls Anne "carrots," and what does Anne do?

Think About the Story:

6. When Marilla makes Anne three "sensible" dresses, Anne tells her she was hoping for one with puffed sleeves and says, "I'd rather look ridiculous when everybody else does than plain and sensible all by myself." What is Anne feeling? Is her statement good or bad?

7. In Chapter 13, Anne tells Marilla:

   "Oh, Marilla, looking forward to things is half the pleasure of them," exclaimed Anne. "You mayn't get the things themselves; but nothing can prevent you from having the fun of looking forward to them. Mrs. Lynde says, 'Blessed are they who expect nothing, for they shall not be disappointed.' But I think it would be worse to expect nothing than to be disappointed."

   Do you agree with Anne or Mrs. Lynde? Why?

8. Name two times Anne has lost her temper, once in these chapters and once earlier. What were the situations?

9. A *paradox* is a statement that seems to contradict itself but is actually true. At the end of Chapter 10, Marilla and Anne have this exchange: "'You shouldn't think so much about your looks, Anne. I'm afraid you are a very vain little girl.' 'How can I be vain when I know I'm homely?' protested Anne." Is Anne vain about her looks? Why or why not? Explain how this might be a paradox.

Dig Deeper:

10. In Chapter 11, what types of rumors start to circulate about Anne before she even attends church for the first time? How does this gossip affect Anne's first visit to Sunday School and church?

11. Why do people gossip? What does the Bible say about gossip? Summarize these verses. Proverbs 11:13, 16:28, and 26:20.

12. After Gilbert offends Anne by calling her "carrots," he says he is sorry, but Anne has decided to hate Gilbert "until death." How does this compare with the time Mrs. Lynde offended her with almost exactly the same comment about her hair?

13. Read Matthew 18:21–22, Mark 11:25, Luke 17:3–4, and Colossians 3:12–14. What does the Bible teach us about forgiveness?

14. From these chapters write a character sketch of Marilla. Is she just, loving, honest, sympathetic? How would you describe her? Has your opinion of Marilla changed since the beginning of the book?

Optional Activities:

1. Anne first encounters her "bosom friend" Diana in Chapter 12. Write two or three paragraphs describing a day that you met a new friend.

2. *Discussion:* Discuss current fashions or popular pastimes that you think kids/teenagers do mostly because of peer pressure. Make certain the finger is not pointed only at "other" groups—what do your groups do that would fit under peer pressure? Do you think it is easy or difficult to recognize things as peer pressure? Does it always get forced on us, or can we do it to ourselves? Is peer pressure always bad? Sometimes innocent? Sometimes good?

3. If weather permits, plan an outdoor picnic; have a picnic indoors if an outdoor picnic is not an option. Have the children bring food that is simple and fun. If possible, have them make it themselves. Serve ice cream.

4. Write about your first day in a new school or your experiences in a new church. Did you feel comfortable and fit in? Did others try to help you feel welcome? How did it compare with Anne's first experiences in church and school?

Chapters 16–22

Vocabulary:

Match each word with its correct definition.

1.	_____ sated	a.	a piece of luggage; a carrying case
2.	_____ tresses	b.	hair
3.	_____ aesthetic	c.	inflexible, relentless
4.	_____ tenacity	d.	to the point; concise
5.	_____ ethereal	e.	satisfied; filled
6.	_____ valise	f.	receptive to beauty
7.	_____ arduous	g.	a brief journey
8.	_____ pithy	h.	enjoyed deep satisfaction
9.	_____ limpid	i.	difficult; daunting
10.	_____ sojourn	j.	heavenly; airy
11.	_____ revelled	k.	contracted, stated
12.	_____ malice	l.	persistence, determination
13.	_____ muse	m.	dreamy meditation
14.	_____ stipulated	n.	ill will, malevolence
15.	_____ inexorable	o.	clear

Questions:

1. How does the fateful mix-up of raspberry cordial and currant wine happen? What is the result?

2. Anne stops attending school for a brief period as a result of Mr. Phillips' unjust treatment. Why does Anne decide to return to class?

3. What motivates Anne to study so very hard?

4. *Alliteration* is a poetic device in which a beginning consonant sound is repeated for dramatic impact, such as *cacophony of crying cats*. Underline words displaying alliteration in this sentence from Chapter 18:

   > The night was clear and frosty, all ebony of shadow and silver of snowy slope; big stars were shining over the silent fields. . . .

   Use alliteration in three sentences of your own.

5. How did Anne know what to do for Minnie May, and what was the result of Anne saving Minnie May's life?

Think About the Story:

6. *Personification* is a literary technique in which a nonhuman object is given human traits. For example, "The breeze playfully ruffled Garrett's hair as it passed over his head." Underline the personification in the following sentence from Chapter 16.

> October was a beautiful month at Green Gables when the birches in the hollow turned as golden as sunshine and the maples behind the orchard were royal crimson and the wild cherry-trees along the lane put on the loveliest shades of dark red and bronzy green, while the fields sunned themselves in aftermaths.

Write your own sentence that includes an example of personification.

7. The happier Anne is, the more she says she feels like praying. Is that the way most people react? When do you pray the most? Read and paraphrase Psalm 28:6–7, Ephesians 6:18, and 1 Thessalonians 5:16–18.

8. In Chapter 20, as Anne walks with Diana to school through Violet Vale, Anne tells her,

    > "Somehow, when I'm going through here I don't really care whether Gil— whether anybody gets ahead of me in class or not. But when I'm up in school it's all different and I care as much as ever. There's such a lot of different Annes in me. I sometimes think that is why I'm such a troublesome person. If I was just the one Anne it would be ever so much more comfortable, but then it wouldn't be half so interesting."

    What makes Anne feel as if she were made up of different Annes? Are there times when you feel as if you were a different person? Why or why not? What changes you the most?

9. In Chapter 22, what is the advice that Marilla gives Anne about good manners and behaving properly? Is this good advice? Why or why not?

Dig Deeper:

10. After forgetting to tell Marilla about the mouse in the sauce and almost having the sauce served to company, why was it like "heaping coals of fire" on Anne's head when Marilla was kind and offered her some strawberry preserves? (Note the allusion to Romans 12:20.)

11. Later, when Anne forgives Mrs. Barry, saying she has no hard feelings, Anne says she feels she has heaped coals of fire on Mrs. Barry's head. What was Anne's motivation in her statement to Mrs. Barry and her comment about heaping coals of fire? Was it right? What should our motivation be? Read Romans 12:17–21.

12. Read Deuteronomy 19:15. How many witnesses were there against Anne for the incident at the tea party? How many witnesses for Anne? Did Mrs. Barry follow these guidelines when she formed her opinion about Anne after the tea party? How important is it that we follow the requirement in Deuteronomy 19?

13. A number of times in these passages, Anne laments that if she does not study hard someone will get ahead of her in school or that if someone finds out about a mishap she will never live it down. Anne never quite says the name of the person she is talking about, however; she starts to, but then changes her words to "the boys" or "some of the others." Who does Anne really mean? What do you think this means?

14. Read Romans 12:17–21 again. How might this passage relate to Anne's actions toward Gilbert Blythe? Use examples from the book to explain your answer.

15.   Read Genesis 37, 39–45. Compare this story with Anne's experiences in Chapter 18. How are the two stories similar? What could each teach us?

16.   Read the section of Chapter 19 where Anne goes to speak to Aunt Josephine and explains that she can imagine how Aunt Josephine felt. Also read Chapter 20 where Anne imagines ghosts. Look at these two situations. What are the consequences of each different use of imagination? Is each use good or bad? Why?

17.   Ever since Anne has arrived at Green Gables, Marilla has been trying to encourage Anne to be a good Christian girl. List three ways in which Marilla tried to instill in Anne an appreciation for Christianity. Were those efforts entirely successful? What, in Chapter 21, causes Anne to think she might like to be a Christian? Why does this new thing have more influence with Anne? Would it have more influence with you?

Optional Activities:

1.   Mrs. Allan is the new minister's wife in Avonlea. She eventually becomes an important role model to Anne. Anne praises her in a variety of ways throughout the book.

> "She's taken our class and she's a splendid teacher. She said right away she didn't think it was fair for the teacher to ask all the questions, and you know, Marilla, that is exactly what I've always thought."

"Mrs. Allan said we ought always to try to influence other people for good. She talked so nice about everything. I never knew before that religion was such a cheerful thing. I always thought it was kind of melancholy, but Mrs. Allan's isn't, and I'd like to be a Christian if I could be one like her."

Do you know someone like this who has had an influence on your life? Write a character sketch of a role model in your life.

2. When an author uses allusions, she assumes that the reader will recognize the allusion and that it will add meaning to the passage. Sometimes, whether because something falls out of fashion or gets lost in time, allusions that mean a lot at one time have less meaning to later readers. In Chapter 17, Montgomery makes an allusion with the following quotation:

> The Caesar's pageant shorn of Brutus' bust
> Did but of Rome's best son remind her more,

See if you can identify the work from which this quotation comes.

3. Research *croup*. Is it still dangerous? Why was it so dangerous to small children? How is it treated?

4. Hold a "concert" similar to the one Anne attends. Have songs and recitations. If you can, find some of the pieces named in the book. Serve refreshments afterward. You may even wish to hold it as a benefit, as they did in Avonlea.

Chapters 23–29

Vocabulary:

An *antonym* is a word that has the opposite meaning of another word. For each of the following words, write its definition, and then underline the antonym in the list that follows the word.

1. **inscrutable:**

   funny
   obvious
   intense
   nervous

2. **shrewish:**

   friendly
   effortless
   strong
   interesting

3. **trifling:**

   thoughtful
   mad
   wailing
   important

4. **laudable:**

   unfathomable
   offensive
   good
   impatient

5. **subjective:**

   clear
   deep
   impartial
   radiant

6. **primal:**

   new
   thoughtful
   concerned
   perplexing

7. **veracity:**

   peace
   wickedness
   lying
   distant

8. **precarious:**

   ornate
   safe
   bright
   rare

9. **prosaic:**

   exciting
   tranquil
   miserable
   swift

10. **aghast:**

    hostile
    complacent
    interested
    water-logged

11. **peerless:**

    visionary
    athletic
    peculiar
    average

12. **pathetic:**

    nimble
    parapet
    invigorating
    nervous

13. **penance:**

    unrepentant
    exhaustion
    merciless
    fury

Questions:

1. What is a ridge-pole? What happens to Anne that involves a ridge-pole?

2. What is a dare? When might a dare be okay and when is it not okay?

3. Why does Anne accept the dare and behave in such a risky manner?

4. Why does Anne write only stories with a "moral purpose"? How does she achieve this? Do you think all stories should be that way?

5. Why do you think Mr. and Mrs. Allan and Aunt Josephine laugh when they read Anne's and Diana's stories?

6. Summarize what happens to Anne's hair.

7. How does Gilbert help Anne in Chapter 28? Why does Anne still refuse his friendship?

Think About the Story:

8. Compare and contrast the teaching styles of Mr. Phillips and Miss Stacy.

9. Marilla grows to develop deep affection for Anne. However, following Anne's triumphant concert performance, Marilla comments:

    "She's a bright child, Matthew. And she looked real nice, too. I've been kind of opposed to this concert scheme, but I suppose there's no real harm in it after all. Anyhow, I was proud of Anne to-night, although I'm not going to tell her so."

    Why does Marilla refuse to openly express her pride in Anne?

10. In Chapter 26, Anne tells Marilla:

    "[Mrs. Allan] said she was a dreadful mischief when she was a girl and always getting into scrapes. I felt so encouraged when I heard that. Is it very wicked of me, Marilla, to feel encouraged when I hear that other people have been bad and mischievous? . . . I'd have thought what an encouraging thing. . . ."

Do you agree with Anne that it can be encouraging to learn that others have done bad things? Why or why not?

11. *Foreshadowing* is the technique of giving hints or clues in a story about something that is coming later. In Chapter 28, Montgomery writes that Anne

> had an odd, newly awakened consciousness . . . that the half-shy, half-eager expression in Gilbert's hazel eye was something that was very good to see. Her heart gave a quick, queer little beat. . . . she was conscious of an odd feeling of regret. She almost wished she had answered Gilbert differently.

What do you think this might foreshadow?

12. At the end of Chapter 28, what does Anne list as shortcomings in herself that she feels she has conquered? What are some shortcomings of your own that you would like to overcome?

13. Why does Matthew urge Anne not to "give up all her romance" at the end of Chapter 28?

14. After finally getting to sleep in a "spare room," Anne says,

> "It was an elegant room, Marilla, but somehow sleeping in a spare room isn't what I used to think it was. That's the worst of growing up, and I'm beginning to realize it. The things you wanted so much when you were a child don't seem half so wonderful to you when you get them."

Do you agree with Anne's opinion? Why or why not? How does this statement compare with what Anne discussed with Marilla (and apparently Mrs. Lynde) near the end of Chapter 13? Were you ever disappointed when something you got was not as you had imagined it? What did you learn?

15. Identify the speaker, context, and significance of this passage from Chapter 29:

> "I'm glad you've got back, I must say. It's been fearful lonesome here without you, and I never put in four longer days.

16. What is an *epoch*? What was Anne's epoch?

Dig Deeper:

17. How does Matthew "spoil" Anne?

18. Read 1 Corinthians 13. Who demonstrates this type of love best, Matthew or Marilla? Use examples from the story to explain your answer.

19. In Chapter 29, Anne states that she believes "it's wrong to do anything you can't tell the minister's wife. It's as good as an extra conscience. . . ." What is our conscience? Why might it be easier to be accountable to someone like Mrs. Allen than to rely on our own conscience?

20. Do you have someone who helps you be accountable for your actions? Who is it and how do they help you?

21. Read John 14:26, Romans 8:26–27, 1 Peter 3:8–17, and James 4:17. What do these verses teach us about our conscience and how it should guide us?

22. When Anne dyes her hair, Marilla exclaims, "'Dyed your hair! Anne Shirley, didn't you know it was a wicked thing to do?'" Anne responds,

> "Yes, I knew it was a little wicked. . . . But I thought it was worth while to be a little wicked to get rid of red hair. I counted the cost, Marilla. Besides, I meant to be extra good in other ways to make up for it."

Is that the way being good works—that we can be "a little" bad if we do other good things? Read James 2:10. What does this verse say about doing something "a little wrong"? How would you feel if a friend thought that it would be okay if she were "a little mean" to you one day if she were a little nicer to you the next?

Optional Activities:

1. An *epiphany* is a moment of sudden awareness, an insight that serves as a turning point for perception, or what we understand. Marilla experiences an epiphany in Chapter 23 when she learns that Anne has fallen from a rooftop.

> At that moment Marilla had a revelation. In the sudden stab of fear that pierced to her very heart she realized what Anne had come to mean to her. She would have admitted that she liked Anne—nay, that she was very fond of Anne. But now she knew as she hurried wildly down the slope that Anne was dearer to her than anything on earth.

Describe a moment of realization from your own life. How did this incident change the way you look at things?

2. Have a class discussion about or write a one- or two-page paper describing an entertaining book you have read that presents a valuable moral theme.

3. *Discussion:* In Chapter 27, Anne buys hair dye from a pedlar who came to the house. Read over the passages in which Anne describes the pedlar, his promises to her, and the sale of the hair dye. Do you think the pedlar mislead Anne on purpose? Do you think everything he said was a deliberate lie, or did he exaggerate only some things, or was he telling the truth as best as he knew it? What can we learn from Anne's experience?

4. What do you think went wrong with Anne's hair dyeing? See if you can discover the problem through research. You may wish to visit a hair salon to see how dyeing is done professionally and ask the hair stylist if he or she can explain what might have gone wrong with Anne's hair.

5. The Exhibition Anne attends with Diana and Aunt Josephine sounds very similar to the exhibits at a county or state fair. If possible, visit a fair and spend some time in the exhibits. You may wish to contact a county agent, or perhaps a local 4-H club, to see if there are exhibits you could enter at the next fair. Perhaps you could organize a small Exhibition in your school or church and raise money for charity or a special cause.

Chapters 30–38

Vocabulary:

Choose eight unfamiliar words from the Word Box. Define each term and use these words in a paragraph.

Word Box

penance	appalled	presentiment	queried
sentiment	aspiration	reproachful	vigour
vivacious	tacitly	sanctifying	unpropitious
rue	anguished	vocation	dubiously
enthralling	calamity	sibilant	scrupulously
perplex	organdy	yore	poised
burnished	brocade	elocutionist	lithe
stolid	languid	nominal	inert
obstinate	vexed	recitation	muslin

Word **Definition**

1.

2.

3.

4.

5.

6.

7.

8.

Paragraph:

_____

_____

_____

_____

_____

_____

_____

_____

_____

_____

_____

_____

_____

_____

_____

_____

Questions:

1. At the beginning of Chapter 30, how does Anne view Marilla's feelings for her?

2. When and why does Miss Stacy criticize Anne's choice of reading material? What does Anne decide to do as a result?

   How do you choose books to read? Read Philippians 4:8. What guidelines does this verse give us in choosing what we read, watch, or listen to?

3. What does Anne finally admit to herself about her feelings for Gilbert? What happens between Anne and Gilbert at the end of the book?

4. When Anne is frozen with stagefright at the Hotel Concert, what is the only thing that saves her?

5. How does Anne's rivalry with Gilbert change during her time at Queen's?

6. In Chapter 31, Anne says to Marilla,

    "[W]hen I'm with you or Mrs. Allan or Miss Stacy I want [to be good] and I want to do . . . what you would approve of. But mostly when I'm with Mrs. Lynde I feel desperately wicked and as if I wanted to go and do the very thing she tells me I oughtn't to do. I feel irresistibly tempted to do it. Now, what do you think is the reason I feel like that?"

    Why do you think Anne feels this way? What does Marilla answer? Have you ever felt as Anne does after receiving good advice? Why or why not?

7. Why does Anne want to do well on her exams? What does she feel will be her sweetest reward if she does well?

8. At the end of Chapter 34, Anne says it is "delightful to have ambitions"; as soon as you achieve one, another lies ahead. Do you agree? Why or why not? What is another word (synonym) for "ambitions"?

9. Why does Marilla consider selling Green Gables?

10.   How does Anne unexpectedly receive a teaching position in Avonlea? How will this affect Gilbert?

11.   What are Anne's two new ambitions?

Think About the Story:

12.   These chapters are full of foreshadowing. Read this excerpt from Chapter 36:

> [Matthew] smiled his shy smile at her as he went into the yard. Anne took the memory of it with her when she went to her room that night and sat for a long while at her open window, thinking of the past and dreaming of the future. Outside the Snow Queen was mistily white in the moonshine; the frogs were singing in the marsh beyond Orchard Slope. Anne always remembered the silvery peaceful beauty and fragrant calm of that night. It was the last night before sorrow touched her life; and no life is ever quite the same again when once that cold, sanctifying touch has been laid upon it.

What is foreshadowed in this passage? Give other examples of foreshadowing in these chapters.

13. Compare Marilla's and Anne's reaction to Matthew's death.

14. After Matthew's death, Anne tells Mrs. Allan, "'It seems like disloyalty to Matthew, somehow, to find pleasure in these things now that he has gone.'" Why does it seem like disloyalty to find pleasure in the world around us after someone special to us has died?

15. What similar experiences have Marilla and Anne had with the Blythe family? How does this seem to affect Anne?

16. Authors often use *symbolism* in their stories; a symbol is an object that stands for a significant, often abstract concept. What does the bend in the road symbolize in the following passage?

> "I don't know what lies around the bend, but I'm going to believe that the best does. It has a fascination of its own, that bend, Marilla. I wonder how the road beyond it goes—what there is of green glory and soft, checkered lights and shadows—what new landscapes—what new beauties—what curves and hills and valleys further on."

Dig Deeper:

17. In Chapter 30 Anne tells Marilla:

> "Miss Stacy. . . . said we couldn't be too careful what habits we formed and what ideals we acquired in our teens because by the time we were twenty our characters would be developed and the foundation laid for our whole future life. And she said if the foundation was shaky we could never build anything really worth while on it."

Later she says,

> "There are so many things to be thought over and decided when you're beginning to grow up. It keeps me busy all the time thinking them over and deciding what is right. It's a serious thing to grow up, isn't it, Marilla? But when I have such good friends as you and Matthew and Mrs. Allan and Miss Stacy I ought to grow up successfully, and I'm sure it will be my own fault if I don't. I feel it's a great responsibility because I have only the one chance. If I don't grow up right I can't go back and begin over again."

Do you agree with Anne? Why or why not? Read Matthew 7:24–27. How does this verse compare with what Anne says?

18. After Anne comes home from Queen's, Matthew says to himself,

> "She's been a blessing to us, and there never was a luckier mistake than what Mrs. Spencer made—if it was luck. I don't believe it was any such thing. It was Providence, because the Almighty saw we needed her, I reckon."

Matthew says that God's hand was at work when Anne arrived at Green Gables. Read Psalm 33:6–15; Matthew 10:29–31; and 1 Peter 5:6, 7. What does the Bible teach about God's providence?

19. Read the following passages and summarize what they say about death. John 3:16–18; 14:1–6; Romans 6:9, 23; 8:38–39; Hebrews 2:14–15; 1 Corinthians 15:50–57; 2 Corinthians 5:1–8.

20. Reread the last two paragraphs of the book. What is Anne's attitude toward her change in circumstances and what lies ahead?

Read Philippians 3:13–14; Ecclesiastes 2:24; 5:18–19; Psalm 121. How do these verses compare to Anne's attitude?

Optional Writing Assignments:

1. A eulogy is a speech that praises an individual and is normally presented at a funeral. Write a eulogy in honor of Matthew Cuthbert. Use details from the book.

2. What are your ambitions or goals for the future? Write a one- to two-page paper listing and explaining your goals.

3. Have you ever lost a loved one? How did you feel? What was hardest for you? What gave you comfort? You may wish to write a letter or a poem or create a picture to communicate your feelings and thoughts.

Essay Projects

Write an essay of one to three pages on some of the following subjects.

1. All literary works include some form of *conflict* or struggle. An *internal conflict* is a struggle inside of a character. An *external conflict* frequently involves problems between individuals. A character's battle against nature would also qualify as an external conflict. Identify and discuss one internal conflict and one external conflict in *Anne of Green Gables*.

2. A *climax* is the high point of action or intensity in a story or its turning point. What is the climax of *Anne of Green Gables*? Explain why you think this is the turning point.

3. How did L.M. Montgomery use humor in *Anne of Green Gables*? How did humor develop Anne's character? Use examples of humor from the story to demonstrate your points.

4. Look up the definitions of *conservative* and *liberal*. How do those terms apply to Rachel Lynde? What is ironic about Rachel Lynde's politics and the way she lives the rest of her life? Use examples from the story to illustrate your answer.

5. A number of characters change, some significantly, during the story of *Anne of Green Gables*. Choose one of the characters and trace the changes that character goes through, using examples from the book to support your opinion.

6. How does Anne serve as a "blessing" to others? In what way are others a blessing to Anne?

7. A reviewer once said of Anne:

> "She was only 11 years old when she reached the house in Prince Edward's Island that was to be her home, but, in spite of her tender years, and in spite of the fact that, excepting for four months spent in the asylum, she had passed all her life with illiterate folks, and had had almost no schooling, she talked to the farmer and his sister as though she had borrowed Bernard Shaw's vocabulary, Alfred Austin's sentimentality, and the reasoning powers of a Justice of the Supreme Court. She knew so much that she spoiled the author's plan at the very outset and greatly marred a story that had in it quaint and charming possibilities"
>
> "A Heroine from an Asylum"
> *New York Times* Saturday Review of Books
> July 18, 1908

Do you agree with the reviewer that Anne Shirley seems too smart to be true? Support your point of view with examples from the book.

8. How does L.M. Montgomery depict religion and God in *Anne of Green Gables*? Use examples from the story to illustrate your opinion.

9. Several times Marilla speaks poorly of people of other ethnic groups: French-Canadian, Italian, German-Jew. Why do you think she does this? Is Marilla intolerant or prejudiced? Does she primarily distrust "outsiders"?

Optional Activities:

1. *Drama:* Create a dramatic adaptation of one chapter or section from the novel. Practice it and present it before the class or at a parent's night.

2. *Poetry recital/Dramatic reading:* Memorize or practice a poem and perform it as Anne did. Use favorite poetry anthologies of your choice.

3. *Speech:* Research women gaining the right to vote. Prepare a five-minute speech about it.

4. *Creative writing:* Write an original poem focusing on nature and it's beauty.

5. *Field Trip:* Visit a botanical gardens or greenhouse. If these are unavailable, spend a field day in the countryside. Identify plants, and sketch them in a nature notebook if desired.

6. *Nature Journal:* Create and maintain a nature journal. Check out one of the following from the library to inspire you. *The Country Diary of an Edwardian Lady,* by Edith Holden; *Keeping a Nature Journal: Discover a Whole New Way of Seeing the World Around You,* by Clare Walker Leslie and Charles E. Roth; and *Wild Days: Creating Discovery Journals,* by Karen Skidmore Rackliffe.

Supplemental Resources

Anne of Green Gables Society

> This organization provides information for Anne enthusiasts of all ages. The $34.00 annual fee includes a subscription to *Kindred Spirits,* a publication devoted to L.M. Montgomery's works.

1-800-665-2663

Kindred Spirits Dept. W
Box 491
Avonlea, Prince Edward Island
Canada
C0B 1M0

www.annesociety.org/secure/society/index.cfm

Anne of Green Gables Museum

> The Anne of Green Gables Museum, located at Silver Bush, Park Corner, Prince Edward Island, allows visitors to view the pastoral surroundings made famous through L.M. Montgomery's fiction. The complex features an antique shop, gift shop, and tearoom in addition to a museum showcasing many of the author's treasured possessions.

1-800-665-2663

Anne of Green Gables Museum
P.O. Box 491, Kensington
C0B 1M0
Prince Edward Island, Canada

www.annesociety.org/Anne

Websites

"Anne Society.org: Kindred Spirits on the Web"

`www.annesociety.org`

>The site's extensive online store includes Anne-related books, dolls, music, stationary, videos, prints, and clothing. A photo gallery displays images of Prince Edward Island locations referenced in the novel.

"*The Avonlea Spectacle*"

`www.avonleaspectacle.com`

>*The Avonlea Spectacle* is a magazine licensed by L.M. Montgomery's family. This exemplary site offers sample articles from the publication.

Other Books by L.M. Montgomery:

Anne of Avonlea (1909)

Anne of the Island (1915)

Anne's House of Dreams (1917)

Anne of Windy Poplars (1936)

Anne of Ingleside (1939)

Emily of New Moon (1923)

Emily Climbs (1925)

Emily's Quest (1927)

Rainbow Valley (1919)

Rilla of Ingleside (1920)

A Tangled Web (1931)

Jane of Lantern Hill (1937)

The Road to Yesterday

The Story Girl

The Golden Road

Books About L.M. Montgomery:

The Alpine Path: The Story of My Career, by L.M. Montgomery (1917)

The Selected Journals of L.M. Montgomery: Volume I (1889–1910), edited by Mary Rubio and Elizabeth Waterston (1985)

Writing a Life: L.M. Montgomery, by Mary Rubio and Elizabeth Waterston (Canadian Biography Series) (1995)

Books of Related Interest:

The Adventures of Tom Sawyer, by Mark Twain

Alice's Adventures in Wonderland, by Lewis Carroll

Heidi, by Johanna Spyri

A Little Princess, by Frances Hodgson Burnett

Little Women, by Louisa May Alcott

Pollyanna, by Eleanor H. Porter

Rebecca of Sunnybrook Farm, by Kate Douglas Wiggin

The Secret Garden, by Frances Hodgson Burnett

Understood Betsy, by Dorothy Canfield Fisher

The Witch of Blackbird Pond, by Elizabeth George Speare

The Wizard of Oz, by L. Frank Baum

Audiobook:

Anne of Green Gables (1987)
> Abridged
> 150 minutes
> Bantam Doubleday Dell Audio Publishing
> Narrated by Megan Follows

Videos:

Anne of Green Gables (1986). Starring Megan Follows, Colleen Dewhurst, and Richard Farnsworth

Anne of Avonlea (1987). Starring Megan Follows and Colleen Dewhurst

Anne of Green Gables: The Continuing Story (2000). Starring Megan Follows

Answer Key

Chapters 1–4

Vocabulary:

1. proper or appropriate actions; 2. an abundant number; 3. of or related to a father or family head; 4. lively; 5. *discerning:* perceptive, *ludicrously:* ridiculous; 6. white; 7. unusual; 8. daydream; 9. bright

Questions:

1. Answers may vary, but should contain some of the following: Anne is imaginative, emotional, impulsive, and talks constantly. Marilla is reserved, crisp, and businesslike. Matthew is quiet, shy, and friendly. Rachel is strong-willed, outspoken, bossy, and nosy.

2. Matthew is 60 years old and is suffering from heart problems. A boy could help with farm chores. Marilla wants to provide the boy with "a good home and schooling."

3. Rachel does not feel that Matthew and Marilla possess adequate experience to raise children. Furthermore, she thinks that orphans may be dangerous.

4. Optimism is the tendency to always look on the bright side of things, to be positive about everything. Accept any reasonable example from the book.

5. Marilla is businesslike and gives Anne little comfort. Anne's chatter and outgoing nature irritate Marilla.

6. Matthew feels compassion for Anne. He finds her "interesting" and would like to provide a good home for her. He thinks he and Marilla could do some good for Anne.

7. Matthew tells Marilla that he thinks they should keep Anne because they could be some good to her, then he becomes silent and just looks at Marilla. He stares wistfully at Anne as Marilla is getting ready to leave and wistfully at the two of them driving away. Mostly, by persistent silent pestering, Matthew is trying to get Marilla's attention and make her give in. The most concrete action he takes is to hire a French boy to help him farm so they won't need an orphan boy.

Thinking About the Story:

8. Word choice and sentences will vary. Possible adjectives are *fringing, darkly, translucent, wavering, wild, white-clad, clear, sweet.*

9. The simile is "like a white-clad girl tiptoeing to her own reflection." New similes will vary.

10. Exodus 22:22–24: God warns us to not harm widows or orphans and declares that he will destroy those who exploit them. Psalm 146:9: The Lord meets the needs of orphans and widow. James 1:27: He wants us, as an act of worship, to take care of orphans and widows.

Dig Deeper:

11. God created nature to be "pleasing to the eye." The magnificence of our world and the heavens shows God's glory. Our Heavenly Father controls all parts of creation. All of creation, including humans, should praise God.

12. Descriptions of Matthew's and Marilla's experiences will differ and answers will vary. In general, Matthew got to spend a lot of time listening to Anne talk about herself and her surroundings in a reasonably calm manner (for Anne). Shortly after Marilla meets Anne, when Anne realizes that Matthew and Marilla wanted a boy, Anne becomes very emotional and dramatic. These experiences probably shaped Matthew's opinion that they could do Anne good by providing a stable home, because he got a better chance to get to know Anne and hear her history. Marilla's opinion—"I don't like children who have so much to say. I don't want an orphan girl, and if I did she isn't the style I'd pick out"—probably comes from Anne's rather confusing emotional fluctuations that first night. Marilla seems to view her as confusing and mildly alarming. Answers will vary concerning whether their reactions are justified.

13. Answers may differ. The situation with Anne and Matthew are actually very similar to the parable of the good Samaritan. Anne could be described as the man who was robbed and beaten—she has virtually no possessions beyond some ugly clothes, she has no home, no one loves her, and she seems to have been taken advantage of for most of her life. Matthew can be seen as parallel to the Samaritan—a most unlikely rescuer, afraid of little girls, not wanting to take in this person, but moved to compassion and action by her need. Matthew shows mercy on Anne as Jesus instructed his followers.

Chapters 5–10

Vocabulary:

Sentences will vary. Definitions follow: 1. benevolent: charitable, kind; 2. blight: a destructive force; 3. harrowed: churned up; 4. tremulous: trembling; 5. penitent: sorry; 6. deprecation: mock, belittle; 7. indignation: anger at perceived slight or unjust act; 8. amiable: pleasant, friendly; 9. abasement: humiliation; 10. plaintive: mournful

Questions:

1. Answers will vary. However, it is true that happiness is an attitude that is influenced by circumstances but not controlled by them. Sometimes it can be true that we are happy or sad because we choose to be.

2. She is embarrassed and says that she is sure they meant to be. Marilla can tell from what Anne says that they were not really good to her, but Anne makes excuses for them.

3. It seems Anne doesn't like to say bad things about others, whether they deserve it or not.

4. Answers will vary. Anne may favor such a location because she can concentrate on God and his creation, because it allows her more scope for her imagination, or because it is peaceful and reflective.

5. Anne's two friends were Katie Maurice and Violetta. Katie Maurice was Anne's reflection in Mrs. Thomas' bookcase door, and Violetta was Anne's echo in a valley outside Mrs. Hammond's place.

6. Matthew convinces Anne to apologize because he misses her company. This incident creates a strong bond between Matthew and Anne.

7. Anne apologizes in a very dramatic way, but she also is sincere. Her apology was in earnest even though she was very dramatic and "revelling in the thoroughness of her abasement."

Think About the Story:

8. Answers and opinions will vary. Imagination can get in the way of dealing with reality—if we imagine things to be different, then we may not work on problems as they really are. But on the other hand, if we cannot imagine things different from the way they are, how can we change things and make them better? Some imagination is necessary to see ways to make things better.

9. Answers will vary. Such a statement leaves things very much up in the air. How can anyone know whether she is being good enough or whether she is trying hard enough? The author does not mention that Anne was bothered by Marilla's conditions, but it seems as if it would make a child afraid of doing the wrong thing—especially a girl like Anne Shirley, who has always been told she is wicked. One of the problems with a statement like this is that there is no objective measure to how good she has to be. One would never know whether she is being good *enough*.

10. According to these verses, because God loves us, we are to love others in the same way Christ loved us. We have a responsibility to show kindness to people, particularly the needy. A natural result of genuine faith is showing Christ's love to others.

11. Answers will vary. In general, both Matthew and Marilla begin the rides assuming Anne will have to return the orphanage and end with each deciding they do not want to send her back. In both rides Anne tells some of her history and takes great delight in her surroundings. They differ in that in the ride with Matthew, Anne thinks she is going to stay at Green Gables but in the first part of the ride with Marilla she thinks she is leaving Green Gables.

12. The reference is an allusion to the Duchess in Chapter 9 of *Alice's Adventures in Wonderland*, by Lewis Carroll. The Duchess in that story spouted a lot of morals that were primarily nonsense ("Everything's got a moral, if only you can find it."). Answers about Montgomery's intent will vary. From Anne's response ("Anne waved the moral inconsequently aside") we might assume that Montgomery is saying Marilla's morals might as well be nonsense for the amount of attention Anne pays. She may also be comparing Anne's situation to Alice's: Anne is in a "wonderland" experience that hardly seems real to her. However, Alice wants to leave and Anne does not. Accept other reasonable answers.

Dig Deeper:

13. Psalm 18:1–2 says our best security is the Lord; he is our rock, shield, and stronghold. Romans 8 tells us that nothing can separate us from the love of God. We can always feel secure in God's care.

14. Answers will vary. She is outspoken and feels that others will always benefit from her advice, so she has a tendency to assume that everything she says is good. She also may not view Anne as someone worthy of respect or care yet. Her attitude toward orphans was not good earlier—she seemed quite willing to believe the worst.

15. We need to speak in love, speak only what is helpful in building others up, and be kind and compassionate. Rachel's comments are not loving or kind. They do not build Anne up.

16. Marilla demands that Anne speak respectfully to Rachel because "she is a stranger and an elderly person and my visitor." Paraphrases will vary but should be similar to this: "Love those who are your enemies and who do bad things to you. Pray for them. Do not fight back. Treat others the way you want to be treated." They are similar to Marilla's statement, but they are even more inclusive. We are to do good to enemies and those who hurt us, treating *everyone* as we would want them to treat us.

17. Answers will vary.

18. Answers will vary. She probably is referring to a kind of rote prayer or recitation versus actually praying what is on one's heart and mind.

Chapters 11–15

Vocabulary:

1. mortified; 2. sallow; 3. sublime; 4. tantalize; 5. beguiled; 6. disdainfully; 7. resolute; 8. bequeathed; 9. brusquely; 10. candidly; 11. vindictive; 12. contritely

Questions:

1. Marilla gives Anne practical dresses that are not pretty. Anne imagines one of them is white muslin with lace frills and puffed sleeves. She also displays her creativity by placing flowers on her plain hat.

2. Marilla recognizes that she feels the same as Anne, she just never admitted it to herself.

3. When Matthew gives chocolates to Anne, she eats one that night and saves the rest to share evenly with her new friend Diana. She finds it "delightful" to be able to offer Diana a gift.

4. Marilla is unable to find her beloved amethyst brooch and blames Anne for its loss. Anne denies losing the brooch, but Marilla decides Anne is lying. Believing that Marilla will allow her to attend the picnic if she confesses, Anne does so. However, she so angers Marilla that Marilla still will not allow her to attend.

5. Gilbert Blythe calls Anne, or her hair, "carrots" to get her attention. Anne hits him over his head with her slate.

Think About the Story:

6. Answers will vary. Anne is feeling the need to fit in, look like the others, belong to a group. She seems to be feeling an unstated peer pressure. The desire to fit in is not wrong, but Anne's statement seems to hint at being willing to do a little too much to fit in: "I'd rather look ridiculous [with] everyone else." On the other hand, the sleeves do *not* look ridiculous to Anne, they look fine. Anne and Marilla seem to be having trouble seeing the other's perspective.

7. Answers will vary. Either idea, taken to its extreme is bad, but both have their merits, too.

8. When Anne is ignoring Gilbert Blythe, he calls her "Carrots." Since Anne is very sensitive about her red hair, she considers the comment a mortal insult. In response, Anne strikes Gilbert in the head with her slate. Earlier Anne lost her temper when Mrs. Lynde said she was skinny, freckled, homely, and had hair as red as carrots.

9. Answers will vary. It could be argued that while Anne may not be vain about her actual appearance, she may be vain about her self-image. This is where paradox would lie, that Anne is so concerned about protecting the image she wishes to portray that she behaves exactly as if she were proud and, as Marilla points out, thinks too much about her looks.

Dig Deeper:

10. People start telling stories about Anne. Mrs. Lynde shares details about Anne's "awful temper," and Jerry Buote labels her "crazy" because she talks to trees and flowers. These tales create negative impressions of Anne. No one at Sunday School makes any friendly advances toward Anne at all.

11. Answers will vary. Sometimes people gossip to make themselves seem important or "in the know"; sometimes to put others down; sometimes just because they want to know everything that is going on; sometimes they have other reasons. Proverbs 11:13: A person who gossips cannot be trusted. Proverbs 16:28: Gossip can ruin close friendships. Proverbs 26:20: Lack of gossip quiets arguments and misunderstandings.

12. Anne refused to forgive or even speak to Gilbert, yet after a short period of anger, she completely forgave Mrs. Lynde.

13. We must forgive others over and over again, with love and peace. We must forgive completely just as God forgives us.

14. Answers will vary. Marilla does not seem very sympathetic and she has a difficult time seeing other people's points of view, particularly Anne's. She seems to view things in very black and white terms, and can appear or act almost cold and hard. However, she clearly loves Anne and is touched by her, though she has a difficult time showing her affection. She is just, though she makes mistakes. She also willingly admits her mistakes and tries to make up for them.

Chapters 16–22
Vocabulary:
1. e; 2. b; 3. f; 4. l; 5. j; 6. a; 7. i; 8. d; 9. o; 10. g; 11. h; 12. n; 13. m; 14. k; 15. c
Questions:
1. When Anne invites Diana to tea, she accidentally serves her currant-wine, which was on the pantry shelf near where the raspberry cordial was *supposed* to be. Mrs. Barry refuses to accept Anne's apology or Marilla's explanation and forbids Diana to ever speak with or play with Anne again.
2. School is the only place where Anne can see Diana during their forced separation and she feels that her studies are all that are left to her.
3. She feels a strong rivalry with Gilbert Blythe, although she won't admit it.
4. Alliteration should include *silver, snowy, slope, stars, silent.* Students may also mark *shadow* and *shining* as complementary sounds. Students' sentences will vary.
5. Anne's years of experience in caring for children prepared her to meet this challenge. The doctor praises Anne's skill and presence of mind that saves Minnie May's life. As a result, Mrs. Barry apologizes to Anne and allows Anne and Diana to play together again.
Think About the Story:
6. Personification in the quotation includes "the lane <u>put on</u> the loveliest shades of dark red and bronzy green," and "the fields <u>sunned themselves</u> in aftermaths." Students' sentences will vary.
7. Answers will vary. Psalm 28: Praise the Lord, trust him, give thanks when you're joyful. Ephesians 6: Pray all the time, in all different ways, and pray for other Christians. 1 Thessalonians 5: Always be joyful, pray all the time, and give thanks in all situations.
8. Different circumstances make Anne feel like different people. Personal answers will vary.
9. She tells Anne to stop thinking of herself and only think of what would be nicest and most agreeable for Mrs. Allan—her hostess. Answers will vary. Anne recognizes it as sound and practical advice and puts it to good use.
Dig Deeper:
10. It is like heaping coals of fire because Marilla is kind and forgiving despite the trouble and embarrassment Anne caused.
11. Answers will vary. Some will see Anne apparently taking pleasure in the guilt Mrs. Barry feels, others may see Anne's comment as simply an observation or perhaps even sympathy. If Anne's motivation was to "heap coals of fire" on Mrs. Barry, then Anne does not seem forgiving inside. True kindness and forgiveness should never want to humiliate or cause further pain to the person you are forgiving. Romans 12:17–21 says we should do what is right, living at peace and overcoming evil with good. Though this passage says this will heap burning coals on an enemy, it does not say this should be our goal. Instead it tells us to "overcome evil with good."
12. The only witness against Anne was Mrs. Barry, who determined that Diana was drunk. The result was not in question, the intent of Anne was at issue. Mrs. Barry did not follow the instruction in Deuteronomy; she concluded from her observation of Diana that Anne intended to get Diana intoxicated. Anne, Diana, and Marilla testified that Anne had no intent to get Diana drunk, that it was an accident. This is a good example of why it is important to rely on the testimony of multiple witnesses and not let emotions or initial impressions form our conclusions.
13. Anne almost says Gilbert, but generally changes to "Gil – some of the others" or something similar. Answers will vary about what this means, but it probably means that Anne thinks about Gilbert a lot and is *very* concerned about what he thinks of her.
14. Answers will vary. Anne makes a point to ignore Gilbert at every opportunity and refuses to be kind. She goes out of her way to compete in school; taunts him with a toss of her head when she beats him; refuses overtures of kindness such as a piece of candy, an apple, and compliments from Gilbert; reads during his public recitation; won't even hear his name mentioned. Actually, Gilbert seems to be following these verses; he goes out of his way to be nice to and compliment Anne. Anne is making a point of not being at peace with Gilbert, she ignores Diana's attempts to make peace, so she is not doing right in people's eyes, and she is not trying to overcome evil with good.
15. The Genesis passages tell the story of Joseph, his sufferings and eventual rise to power and rescue of his family. The history and experiences of Joseph and Anne are parallel in that both went through suffering and degradation, but were able to use their experiences to save lives and rise above their pasts and not hold grudges (not counting Gilbert Blythe).

Personal applications will vary, but the general idea should be that we may not understand present suffering, but that we can learn from everything that happens to us. We never know how things may work out and eventually be used for good.

16. Answers will vary. In Aunt Josephine's case, Anne is able to imagine herself in Aunt Josephine's position, and helps Aunt Josephine see the other side of the experience by imagining herself in the girls' position. In Chapter 19, Anne and Diana have imagined things so well that they now believe the woods to be truly haunted and cannot go there after dark. In the first case, imagination is good because it helps them to picture themselves as someone else and see their perspective. In the case of the woods, the imagination is bad because the girls made something appear real that wasn't and caused fear. The first imagination was liberating, the second imagination was controlling and entrapping.

17. Examples of Marilla trying to instill an appreciation of Christianity in Anne will vary, but may include making Anne say her prayers, making her memorize the Lord's Prayer, sending her to church and Sunday School, not allowing her to speak badly of others. More may apply. The efforts had some influence on Anne, but it was not until Mrs. Allan, the new pastor's wife, came that Anne expressed real interest in being Christian: "I'd like to be a Christian if I could be one like her." This seems to be because Mrs. Alan demonstrates true love and joy—she is an example of someone who is "glad she's a Christian," as opposed to Mr. Bell, who "doesn't seem to get any comfort out of it." Personal answers will vary.

Optional Activities:
2. The quotation is from *Childe Harold's Pilgrimage,* Canto 4, by George Gordon Byron.

Chapters 23–29
Vocabulary:
1. inscrutable: mysterious; antonym: obvious; 2. shrewish: ill-tempered; antonym: friendly; 3. trifling: trivial, unimportant; antonym: important; 4. laudable: worthy of praise; antonym: offensive; 5. subjective: individual judgment; antonym: impartial; 6. primal: fundamental, early, primitive; antonym: new; 7. veracity: truthfulness; antonym: lying; 8. precarious: dangerous; antonym: safe; 9. prosaic: dull, unimaginative; antonym: exciting; 10. aghast: shocked; antonym: complacent; 11. peerless: matchless, special, incomparable; antonym: average; 12. pathetic: sad, moving; antonym: invigorating; 13. penance: an action showing sorrow or repentance; antonym: unrepentant

Questions:
1. A ridge-pole is the beam in the roof to which rafters are attached. In this case it may also refer to a long board or metal strip that caps the peak of the roof. Anne accepts a dare and tries to walk a ridge-pole. She falls and breaks her ankle.

2. A dare is a challenge by someone else to do something out of the ordinary. Answers will vary, but may mention that dares to do something dangerous, mean, or wrong should not be made or accepted.

3. Anne is trying to impress her friends. She does not want to appear fearful and wants to maintain her "honour."

4. Anne says she wants her stories to have a "wholesome effect" on readers. Anne's stories feature rewards for "good people" and punishments for "all the bad ones." Opinions will vary. Although it is wrong to encourage or promote being bad, it is also not realistic to *always* show the good people getting rewarded and the bad people being punished.

5. Answers will vary. They may find them naïve or overly dramatic. It is certain that they enjoyed them; they did not seem to find the stories poorly written.

6. Anne's hair turns green when she uses dye purchased from a peddler. She had been trying to dye it black. The green will not wash out, so Marilla has to cut Anne's hair very short. The experience apparently teaches Anne to be much more satisfied with her looks.

7. While Anne is reenacting a dramatic death scene from *Idylls of the King,* by Alfred, Lord Tennyson, her small boat sinks, and she has to leap from the boat to a bridge piling. Gilbert comes by in a boat and rescues her from the bridge piling to which she is clinging. She nurses her grudge by recalling to her mind the wrong he had done to her so that she would not waiver in hatred.

Think About the Story:
8. Miss Stacy is Avonlea's new schoolteacher. Though Mr. Phillips frequently embarrassed and frustrated his students and spent almost all his time paying attention to one particular student, Miss Stacy stimulates and encourages all her pupils. For example, Miss Stacy makes education exciting by taking her class on field trips to study nature. Miss Stacy's sweet and pleasant spirit motivates her students to perform well in the classroom.

9. Answers will vary. Marilla seems to be unused to expressing affection and pride, she seems to feel it is more important to guard against vanity than it is to nurture, and she seems to value plain, practical things and actions.

10. Answers will vary. Sometimes it can be encouraging, as Anne says, to know that we can rise above those actions or outgrow them. It can also be helpful to learn that we are not the only ones to struggle with certain problems.

11. Answers will vary. In actuality, Anne and Gilbert become fast friends at the end of the book, and Anne spends the intervening chapters deeply regretting that she so vehemently rejected Gilbert after his help and offer of friendship.

12. She feels she has conquered meddling with things that don't belong to her, letting her imagination run away with her, carelessness in cooking, vanity, and being too romantic. Answers will vary.

13. Answers will vary.

14. Answers will vary. It is often true that we are disappointed when we actually get something we desired because often it is hard for reality to live up to imagination—we generally don't imagine any troubles or problems will come with our desires! This happens at every age, not just adulthood. Near the end of Chapter 13, Marilla said "'I'm afraid there'll be a great many disappointments in store for you through life,'" and Mrs. Lynde said, "'Blessed are they who expect nothing, for they shall not be disappointed.'" Answers will vary, but perhaps Anne is learning that there is some wisdom in not setting expectations *too* high, and it is never good to base your happiness on whether things are what you expected them to be. Personal examples will vary.

15. Marilla says this to Anne when Anne returns home after attending the Exhibition and visiting Aunt Josephine. The statement is significant because Marilla openly displays affection for Anne and admits she missed her.

16. An epoch is an event that begins a new period of time in one's life. Anne's epoch was staying at Miss Barry's and going to the exhibition.

Dig Deeper:

17. Throughout the novel, Matthew brings Anne special treats and praises her talents. In Chapter 25, Matthew decides to purchase a beautiful dress for Anne's Christmas gift. Most importantly, Matthew's unconditional love and approval provides Anne with security.

18. 1 Corinthians 13 says love is patient, kind, and focused on the needs of others; is linked to truth and hope; and perseveres and is eternal. Matthew seems to demonstrate this kind of love more than Marilla. He is very patient, is always willing to listen, sacrifices for her (buying the dress and facing the woman clerk!), believes her, and encourages her. Marilla is more apt to jump to the conclusion that Anne is late or wrong or lying, tends to be impatient, and is unwilling to compliment her. Note that this does *not* mean Marilla does not love Anne, just that she is not good at expressing it.

19. Our conscience is the small voice in our head that tells us when we are doing wrong. Answers will vary. Sometimes we can make excuses in our heads for why something might be right or wrong, but we generally can tell whether someone else would really approve of our actions.

20. Answers will vary. Anne's romance is part of what makes her unique and exciting.

21. These verses tell us that God gave us the Holy Spirit to teach us things and remind us of all that Jesus said. The Holy Spirit helps us in our weaknesses, and prays for us. Do good and be peaceful for God watches us, be prepared to explain your reason for hope (Christ) and keep a clear conscience. If we know what we ought to do and we don't do it, we have sinned.

22. Being good is not a seesaw we are trying to keep level so that our good is balanced with our bad. James says if we sin in one thing then we have sinned in everything; if we break just one part of the law we are lawbreakers. It is not okay to rob a bank even if we promise to not speed as we drive away, or even if we plan to give part of the money to the poor! Answers will vary about the friendship question, but probably will be "no."

Chapters 30–38
Vocabulary:

Word definitions follow: *penance:* An act of self-mortification or devotion performed voluntarily to show sorrow for a sin or other wrongdoing. *appalled:* Filled with consternation or dismay. *presentiment:* A sense that something is about to occur; a premonition. *queried:* To express doubt or uncertainty about; question. To put a question to someone. *sentiment:* A thought, view, or attitude, especially one based mainly on emotion instead of reason. *aspiration:* A strong desire for high achievement. An object of such desire; an ambition. *reproachful:* Expressing reproach or blame. *vigour:* Physical or mental strength, energy, or force. Strong feeling; enthusiasm or intensity. *vivacious:* Full of animation and spirit; lively.

tacitly: Not spoken, silent. Implied by or inferred from actions or statements. *sanctifying:* Setting apart for sacred use; consecrate. To make holy; purify. *unpropitious:* Unfavorable; inauspicious. *rue:* To feel regret, remorse, or sorrow. *anguished:* Agonizing physical or mental pain; torment. *vocation:* A regular occupation, especially one for which a person is particularly suited or qualified. A calling. *dubiously:* Fraught with uncertainty or doubt; undecided. *enthralling:* To hold spellbound; captivate. *calamity:* An event that brings terrible loss, lasting distress, or severe affliction; a disaster. *sibilant:* Of, characterized by, or producing a hissing sound like that of (s) or (sh). *scrupulously:* Conscientious and exact; painstaking. *perplex:* To confuse or trouble with uncertainty or doubt. *organdy:* A stiff transparent fabric of cotton or silk, used for trim, curtains, and light apparel. *yore:* Time long past. *poised:* Assured; composed. Held balanced or steady in readiness. *burnished:* To make smooth or glossy by rubbing. A smooth glossy finish or appearance; luster. *brocade:* A heavy fabric interwoven with a rich, raised design. *elocutionist:* A person with the art of public speaking in which gesture, vocal production, and delivery are emphasized. *lithe:* Readily bent; supple. Marked by effortless grace. *stolid:* Having or revealing little emotion or sensibility; impassive. *languid:* Showing little or no spirit or animation; listless. Lacking vigor or force; slow. *nominal:* Insignificantly small; trifling. *inert:* Unable to move or act. Sluggish in action or motion; lethargic. *obstinate:* Stubbornly adhering to an attitude, opinion, or course of action; obdurate. Difficult to manage, control, or subdue; refractory. *vexed:* Irritated, distressed, or annoyed. *recitation:* The act of reciting memorized materials in a public performance or the material so presented. *muslin:* Any of various sturdy cotton fabrics of plain weave, used especially for sheets. Paragraphs will vary but should be consistent with these definitions.

Questions:

1. Anne "had no idea how Marilla loved her." She felt Marilla "was very hard to please and distinctly lacking in sympathy and understanding." However, she also appreciated all Marilla had done for her.

2. Miss Stacy finds Anne reading *The Lurid Mystery of the Haunted Hall,* "a very silly unwholesome book." Anne acknowledges the novel's flaws and decides to ask Miss Stacy or Mrs. Allan to approve all future novels. Personal answers will vary. According to the Philippians passage, we should try to concentrate on things that are noble, right, pure, lovely, and admirable.

3. In Chapter 30, Anne admits to herself that she has forgiven Gilbert. Later she begins to admire Gilbert and wishes they could be friends. In the last chapter, Anne and Gilbert finally become friends after Gilbert gives up his teaching job in Avonlea so Anne will be able to teach there. Gilbert walks Anne home and they talk for a long time outside Green Gables.

4. Anne spots Gilbert smiling and she thinks he is laughing at her. She can't bear the thought of Gilbert laughing at her.

5. Even though Anne still energetically battles Gilbert for academic honors, she no longer harbors feelings of anger against him. Anne's focus becomes positive; instead of wanting to beat Gilbert as a form of revenge, she longs to meet her own potential and treats her rivalry with Gilbert only as a challenge.

6. Answers will vary. Marilla says sometimes she feels the same way. She tells Anne that Rachel is a good woman and means well, but that her nagging doesn't make people want to do good. Personal answers will vary.

7. Anne wants to please Matthew. Matthew claims that Anne will "beat the whole Island," and she wishes to reward his unwavering confidence in her abilities. Her sweetest reward will be seeing Matthew's eyes gleaming with pride in her achievement.

8. Answers will vary. Another word for "ambitions" is "goals," which is more commonly used now. It is good to have goals; they give us direction and a way to measure our progress in life.

9. The bank in which Marilla and Matthew kept their money has failed, and all their money is gone. In addition, Matthew had taken out several loans the previous fall and they must be repaid. Marilla fears that her potential blindness will leave her essentially helpless and she will be unable to keep up the house and property, even with a good hired hand.

10. Gilbert withdraws his application and recommends to the school board that Anne receive the local position. As a result, Gilbert will have to pay for lodging in a different town while attempting to save money for college.

11. She is going to be a good teacher and save Marilla's eyesight.

Think About the Story:

12. The death of Matthew is foreshadowed in this scene. Matthew's death is also foreshadowed by mentions of his heart trouble and the way he looked after Anne returned home. Marilla's eye trouble is foreshadowed by her headaches. The bank failure is foreshadowed by Marilla asking Anne about the bank's stability. Anne's reconciliation with Gilbert might be foreshadowed by Marilla's account of her old relationship with Gilbert's father.

13. Uncharacteristically, Marilla expresses her emotions freely and loudly, and for the first time she tells Anne how much she loves her. Anne wishes to be alone and cannot cry, but only feels a dull, empty ache until she wakes up in the middle of the night; then she cries and clings to Marilla for comfort.

14. Answers will vary, but Mrs. Allan tells her we resent the idea that things can or should please us when someone we love is no longer here to share the pleasure, and we feel unfaithful to our sadness when we become interested in life again.

15. Marilla once had a very good relationship with John Blythe, Gilbert's father—people him called her beau (boyfriend). However, Marilla had a fight with John and refused to forgive him though he asked her to, and their relationship was destroyed. Marilla has always regretted it. Marilla may be advising Anne to make up with Gilbert before it's too late; her story certainly seems to influence Anne to make up with Gilbert later.

16. Answers will vary. The road is a common symbol in literature for one's life or the future. The bend in the road represents a major change in Anne's life, beyond which she cannot see. Anne planned to pursue advanced studies at Redmond. However, she sacrifices her prestigious scholarship to meet Marilla's needs. Anne's optimistic outlook allows her to view this bend in the road with enthusiasm for the future.

Dig Deeper:

17. Answers will vary. Anne's words are very similar to Jesus' in Matthew 7. Jesus says that we must understand and live by his words to build a good foundation for our lives because our ideas and actions often set a pattern for our later life.

18. Answers will vary. Psalm 33: God made and controls everything and he considers all that we do. Matthew 10: God knows and is concerned about the smallest details about us. 1 Peter: We should be humble before God and give him our worries because he cares for us.

19. John 3:16–18: Belief in Jesus Christ as savior and lord saves us from eternal death. John 14:1–6: Jesus prepares a place for us in heaven when we believe in him. Romans 6:9: Christ triumphed over death. Romans 6:23: Death is a consequence of sin. Romans 8:38–39: Nothing, not even death, can separate us from God. Hebrews 2:14–15: Christ frees his children from the fear of death. 1 Corinthians 15:50–57: All who believe in Jesus will be changed and immortal; and death will lose its victory. 2 Corinthians 5:1–8: When we leave our earthly body, we will be home with Jesus in heaven if we believe.

20. Answers may vary. Anne recognizes that things have changed for her and she no longer has all the options for her life that she had before. But she is satisfied with that and also recognizes that there will be plenty of joy and happiness along the path she has chosen. She is content with her choice and looks forward to the future. These verses advise us to forget what is behind, press forward toward the goal; find satisfaction in our work and be happy; look up to God and trust in him; he will care for us and watch over us. Anne seems to be following this advice.